T0355051

More Than Words

DARON KENNETH

authorHOUSE

AuthorHouse™
1663 Liberty Drive
Bloomington, IN 47403
www.authorhouse.com
Phone: 833-262-8899

© 2022 Daron Kenneth. All rights reserved.

No part of this book may be reproduced, stored in a retrieval system, or transmitted by any means without the written permission of the author.

Published by AuthorHouse 11/08/2022

ISBN: 978-1-6655-7396-2 (sc)
ISBN: 978-1-6655-7397-9 (e)

Print information available on the last page.

Any people depicted in stock imagery provided by Getty Images are models, and such images are being used for illustrative purposes only. Certain stock imagery © Getty Images.

This book is printed on acid-free paper.

Because of the dynamic nature of the Internet, any web addresses or links contained in this book may have changed since publication and may no longer be valid. The views expressed in this work are solely those of the author and do not necessarily reflect the views of the publisher, and the publisher hereby disclaims any responsibility for them.

Contents

A Life Obscure

Some days all I do is cry
And still I don't know just why
I have to live my life this way
So sad and so very full of pain.
SomeTymes I wish that I was dead
And free from the demons in my head.
I cry someTymes all day and night
This way of living isn't right.
I don't know which way to turn
When I wish I was ashes in an urn.
There are Tymes when I just feel so weak
I haven't got the courage to speak.
So I watch the tears fall to the floor
I don't' want to live this way anymore.
SomeTymes it's hard to make it through
When depression leaves you feeling so blue.
There are Tymes when I wish I wasn't alive
It's so hard to watch the world turn and thrive.
I get so sad that I wish my life was over
This makes it hard to live my life sober.
Each day I thank God for my husband and pet
For without them I wouldn't be here yet.
One day I hope they find a cure
So I can leave behind this life obscure.

I'm feeling lost and feeling low
I don't know how much lower I can go.
I'm feeling down and feeling bad
This depression has me here feeling sad.
I don't know how to get out of this hole
It's tearing away at the heart of my soul.
I'm falling down and falling fast
I just can't seem to avoid the past.
The past I face, it brings me down
It has my head spinning all around.
I'm feeling down and feeling depressed
I'm feeling like a total mess.
I take my meds, I take my pills
They never seem to cure my ills.
So I cry, yes I cry, though I don't know why
I feel like damaged goods deep inside.
I'm just so tired of being insane.
I'm so tired of feeling all this pain.
I wish I could change the way that I feel
I'm so tired of living a life that's surreal.

A mother's Love is unconditional. It is the kind
Of stuff of dreams. A mother Loves their children
Irregardless of the things that they do...good and
Bad. A mother's Love begins at birth and stays
With her children their life long. Many Tymes has
A mother told her children just how she feels in a
Greeting card, a hug or just plain words that she
Uses to talk to her children over the years. When
Her children are very young she is their guardian
Keeping them safe from harms way and the situa-
Tions that require her to watch over the things that
Her children do. As her children she is their teacher
Teaching them the life lessons that they need to
Know, how to walk, how to talk and hoe to behave
Properly in all of life's situations. As her children
Grow, they continue to learn from her, like how to
Cook and clean for themselves. As her children
Become young adults, she teaches them the things
That they will need to know when they leave their
Home and venture out into the world. As they
Begin to have families of their own she continues
To Love the children her children have of their own.
Quite simply put, a mother's Love is forever.

Alone

I woke up today, I'm feeling so down
My smile now is replaced by a frown.
I really wish that I was feeling better
My mood is just as bad as the weather.
I hope that one day soon, that I'll be fine
The only help I'll get is from the divine
I ask him just why I must live this way
I guess that there's just not much for Him to say.
So I turn my attention way up to the sun,
I hope that one day soon I'll be having some fun
The way I feel is really low
The way that I move is rather quite slow
There's not much lower that I can go
I'll have to make it through all alone.
So now I turn myself around
It feels like all of my limbs are now bound.
So now I try to pray to God,
I only feel like I'm just a clod.
I hope that I'll feel better tomorrow
And get away from all of this sorrow.
I don't feel happy inside of my head
I'm starting to feel like I wish I was dead.
Maybe someday soon my moods will change
And in my life I'll try to rearrange
The way I feel is really low
The way that I move is rather quite slow
There's not much lower that I can go
I'll have to make it through all alone.

Billy, Georgia and Laurie

Billy, Georgia and Laurie are my cousins on my
Father's side of the family. Growing up, my sister
And I spent countless hours and days at their house
And them at ours. They never felt like cousins, but
More like an extended family of brothers and sisters.
We would often spend nights at their house and they
At our house. We grew up together and built a wonder-
Ful bonding experience over the many years we had in
Elementary through high school. I know I speak for
Them when we said we Loved them like family. Billy
And Georgia were two and four years younger than I
Am respectively. Laurie was the eldest of us. She spent
Many nights babysitting us. She was the best babysitter
You could ever wish for. She always made sure that we
Were safe and didn't get into any trouble. As we got
Older the roles changed and I began to baby sit us as
Laurie got older and spent more Tyme with her friends.
We always had the best Tymes just playing and spending
Tyme together. As we got older we stopped spending as
Much Tyme together but continued to Love and cherish
Them as our own family. As we've gotten older we don't
See each other as much but I know that they will always
Be the brother and sisters we Loved so very dearly and
So very, very much.

Brown Eyes

Brown eyes you're handsome and you're mine
You've got me singing all the Tyme
You lift me up when I'm low down
You help to chase away my frown
I'm so glad that you're my friend
We'll be together till the end
Come now take me by the hand
You've got me feeling oh, so grand
We can go for a little walk
And while we do we can talk
About our future and what it holds
Your friendship means more to me than gold
I like the way we always get along
You cheer me up when things go wrong
I so Love it when we spend Tyme together
You can cheer me up despite the weather
If there's just one thing that I could do
I'd help you to feel the same way too.

Carol and Sue

Whether I'm with Carol or my friend Sue
We always find really cool things to do.
We have fun when we go for a ride
While just taking in sun makes us feel alive.
SomeTymes we just sit on the porch in the afternoon
While at night we take in all the stars and the moon.
We get together when we have bad weather
It's always nice just to get together.
Often Tymes we have fun just cooking up treats
It's always nice to stay in or to go out to eat.
We can get together for hours and talk
Or even have fun just going for a walk.
We can enjoy going from store to store
Having fun with them is never a bore.
We enjoy touring around the city
Taking in the sites is really quite nifty.
SomeTymes we just sit and talk on the phone
Just talking is better than being alone.
We can enjoy just going to a park or zoo
Doing things together makes you feel brand new.
We can have fun just enjoying a beach
Having fun doesn't have to feel out of reach.

Cotton Tail

I look out to the backyard
I see a little bunny,
The way he gently moves
Is rather sort of funny.

He watches as I look at him
He looks for food all around,
His tail is white like cotton
His fur is shades of brown.

When he's in the backyard
I'll put carrots out for him to eat,
He's really quite a character
He's rather cute and sweet.

He can hop all over
He nibbles on the grass,
He can move quite quickly
He jumps around so fast.

If I get too close to him
He'll hop back to his hutch,
I hope we can be friends one day
Because I like him oh, so much.

Crimson and Gold

The leaves are now turning
From crimson to gold,
The chilly Fall air
Leaves us feeling quite cold.
We push all of the leaves
Into a great big pile.
We jump into them
It makes us all smile.
The seasons change
From Fall to Winter
We burn leaf piles
Into ash and cinder.
The air outside
Is cold and crisp,
The clouds above
Form into a wisp,
And late in the night
We'll see the bright moon,
We know that change
Will be here quite soon.
So try to enjoy
Each last Fall day
Because we know
Winter's soon on its way.

Dana, Dearest

Except for her cat, she lives by herself
She has pictures of memories that she keeps on a shelf.
She's close to her mom, and also to her brother
She once had a girlfriend that she called her Lover.
She used to be outgoing, now she's kind of shy
She wishes she had someone to talk to as days roll by.
She remembers when once she had lots of friends
Those days are now long gone, they never seem to end.
She sits alone waiting for the telephone to ring
For someone to talk to she'd do most anything.
She fears open spaces despite of its stigma
Just how she gets by is still quite an enigma.
Those people that who knew her, now say she's too thin
She looks like a skeleton that's covered up with skin.
Without any help, she'll soon fade away
She'll just be another statistic on another lonely day.

Dirty Dog

You treat our mother like she's a dirty dog
Stop living your life like a hog.
It's such a nasty thing for you to do
Do something for someone else but you.
I can't stand the way you treat our mother
You treat her like she's just a bother.
Stop treating her like she's just a pest
You need to clean up your own mess.
You can't even take out your own trash
You're nasty like a rotten rash.
It's Tyme for you to get your cleaning done
You need to finally get up off your bum.
You take advantage of her every day
It's Tyme for you to stop acting in this way.
You need to stop being so rude
And knock off being so crude.
So put your pity pride on the shelf
And think of someone besides yourself.
All you ever do is think of who you can use
The way you play this game you're bound to lose.
You won't be happy until the day she's gone
You'll finally have to do things on your own.
You really need to get yourself together
Take some medicine and you'll be better.

So many years have come and gone
Still to depression I remain a pawn.
I remember all the years of sadness
That to this day still lead to madness.
I remember the days that I just cried
I had just wished that I would have died.
I can't stand to feel this way
I still have so much to say.
But those who really know me
Aren't surprised by what they see.
Some days I just feel so sad
It really hurts to feel so bad.
Some days I wish I'd never wake
SomeTymes it gets too much to take.
There are days where I just cry alone
Where I can do nothing but stay ay home.
It's in this world that I don't fit in
I still can't remember just where I've been.
Wherever I go I leave sadness behind
As proof that I once had an intelligent mind.
One day I hope they find a cure
So I can leave behind this life obscure.

Down

I'm so tired of living life sober,
I feel like most of my life is now over.
I just feel a life here in pain
And that I'm filled with so much disdain.
I wish that I could crack a smile
And just feel better for a little while.
I'm so tired of feeling so low,
I don't know how much lower I can go
The life I've been living is way too dark,
I feel like my life has lost it's spark,
I try to speak but only bark,
This depression has left it's lonely mark.
No it's not easy to live life sober
Especially when my happiness is now over.
I'm so tired of living with so much pain
And live a life that's full of so much disdain.
So now I try to force a smile
And hopefully feel better for even a while
I'm so sick of living so low
There's not much further that I can go.
The life I've been living is much too dark
My life has lost it's only spark,
I try to speak but only bark
This depression has left it's lonely mark.
I'll never make it living life sober
My days of happiness are now over
I'm so sick of living with all this pain
I can only live with so much disdain,
I try hard but never see a smile
It's been this way now for a while
There's not much further I can go,
I wish I didn't feel so low.

Down Day

I woke up feeling down today
I wish I didn't feel this way
No, I hoped that I'd feel good
And that I was in a better mood
I'm so tired of feeling low
There's not much lower I can go
Until I finally reach the bottom
I'm so sick of feeling rotten
So I called my friend up on the phone
I was so surprised he wasn't home
I wish that I could talk to him
And get out of this mood I'm in
He always has nice things to say
That put me in a better way
I wish I didn't feel so tired
Someday soon I'll be too wired
Yes someday soon I'll be feeling manic
When I do I'll start to panic
I long to be somewhere in the middle
Why I can't is such a riddle
I'm always low or way too high
I wish this day would fly on by
I wish my moods changed like the weather
I hope someday soon that I'll feel better.

As he lays there on his bed, his stomach rises up
And down. Every once in a while he will let out
A meow which tells me he is in dream mode. As
His belly rises and falls he keeps an eye on what
Is going on around him. His soft furry ears perk
Up to the many different sounds in the house.
The constant rising and falling of his chest and
Belly helps me to relax. Up and down...up and
Down. When he starts meowing loudly I know
That he is having a dream. I often wonder what
Is going on in that cat mind of his. I am so glad
That he is able to fall asleep and dream in our
House. Some of my other cats never purred or
Meowed when they were asleep which led me
To wonder if they were asleep and dreaming or
Just asleep. As soon as he wakes up he begins
The job of washing himself. Often then he just
Falls back to sleep. SomeTymes he comes over
And rubs his head against my leg. This is a sign
That he wants cat treats which I give him...and
Then its off to wash and then right back to sleep.
He has such a rough life...eat,wash sleep repeat.
Eat, wash sleep repeat...eat, wash sleep repeat!

You always lend me a helping hand
Your Love makes me feel so grand
You know I speak the truth to you.

You're always so good to me
Your Love is all I need to see
On these days that I live through.

You're the kindest man I know
You help my moods to even flow
In these Tymes when life is tough.

You're my closest friend
You'll be there till the end
When things get to be so rough.

You're better than all the rest
You always give your best
I never get enough of you.

You're as gentle as a dove
You're the man I Love
You're all I think about it's true.

You're the man who always tries so hard
You're my good luck charm
We'll spend eternity together.

You're my family man
You always do the best you can
I'll Love you forever.

SomeTymes I don't know just what to do
When I get to feeling so sad and blue.
I get so sad all I do is cry
It makes me feel like I want to die.
I feel like I'll never feel better
I even feel bad when we have good weather.
When I feel low I call my friends
I feel like I've reached the end.
I wish my sadness would just go away
I wonder if I'll make it through the day.
I feel like I don't want to eat
It feels like my body's been beat.
When I get down I don't feel good
Nothing feels just like it should.
I sit all alone in a darkened room
And I get so sick of all this gloom.
I remember to take all of my meds
To cure this sadness in my head.
I just can't take the way it's been
I hope one day soon I'll feel good again.

Today is a day that I feel so sad
I don't know why I'm feeling so bad
I wish I felt more like myself
And leave my sadness on a shelf
I get so low I start to cry
Though I don't know just why
I'm tired of living my life so low
I don't think there's much lower I can go
When I get low I seek out my friends
Just hoping they can help my sadness end
I want to be happy and lose this sadness
I'm tired of living a life of madness
It's hard to live a life of depression
I wish I could find some sadness suppression
I take my pills to fight how I feel
When it gets like this it's so surreal
I pray some prayers to God above
And hope he'll turn my sadness to Love
So until that day that I'm feeling good
I'll stay in therapy like I should.

Feeling the Blues

It isn't easy when you always feel blue
I never know just what I should do
To make the sadness go away
And help to keep my depression at bay.
I remember when I used to smile
I haven't felt that way in a while.
SomeTymes all I can do is cry
Though I don't know the reason why.
If I'm sad I count to ten
If I'm still sad I do it again.
I know I need to take my meds
When they don't work I just go to bed.
It feels like it's raining in my brain
It feels like it's going to rain again.
When I get down my body aches
SomeTymes it gets so hard to take.
When I get down, I get so tired
And when I'm manic I get so wired.
SomeTymes it helps to talk to friends
But my brain it never seems to mend
SomeTymes I want to scream aloud
I feel all alone even in a crowd.
I don't like it when I get manic
It puts me in a state of panic.
I often feel really full of dread
I hope I'm cured before I'm dead.

For Susan

I guess now that it's over
We had a tiff that's true
We went our separate ways
But life isn't the same without you.
So I sit alone
And wish that you were here
Nothing feels the same
I miss you oh, my dear.
I hear words inside my mind
I only hope what they say is real
I sit alone and pray
You'll hear the words I speak and feel.
We used to spend our Tyme together
Now I spend my Tyme alone
There are so many things I'd like to say
If I could get you on the phone.
Please just give me one more chance
I feel so alone and I feel sad
I know you're hurting also
It's not cool to feel so bad,
So I spend my Tyme in sadness
A shell of my former self
I feel like my life is over
And I'm sitting somewhere on a shelf.
If by chance you find me
Please take a hold of me with care
And rock me oh, so gently
Then put me back up there.

We've had Shadow now for four glorious years…He's
Ones of the most wonderful pets we have had the joy
Of owning. He was a rescue when we first got him and
He was very timid. Whenever someone would try to pet
Him or show him some affection he would lash out and
Bite them. For the longest Tyme he just kept to himself,
But slowly he began to trust us and he began to sit with
Us when we were in the living room. He never sat on
My lap but he felt comfortable enough to let us brush
Him and watch T.V. with us. But today was an exceptional
Day. For the first Tyme since we've had him he actually
Came up and sat on my lap. This may not sound like a
Big deal but it was to me. He only stayed on my lap for
Ten minutes but he did lat me pet and brush him while he
Sat on my lap. He stared into my eyes while I told him
Just how much I Love him. It was truly a long Tyme in
The making. It was one of the nicest experiences I have
Ever known. I hope he continues to trust us and share in
This wonderful bonding experience again.

He Is the King

I look up in the air
I see an eagle as he flies,
He moves with his great stealth
Then he let's out his cries.
He cries out as he soars,
He flies above the land,
He looks so stark and strong,
He's regal and so grand.
He scours above the waters
He searches for his food,
He catches mice and fish
Then feeds them to his brood.
After he's caught his meal
He'll fly back to his nest,
He'll tear apart his meal
He eats with zeal and zest.
He sees with his keen eyes
He flies with his broad wings,
He'll soar above the land
Of birds he is the king.

He's a Good Boy

He sleeps a lot, then he starts to snore
There's no way I could Love him more.
He's so cute with his golden eyes
He snuggles up to me to my surprise.
He's so clean he always gives himself a bath
He's quite silly and he makes me laugh.
He likes to watch the animals outside
He plays a game where he likes to hide.
He always has a black, wet nose
He has webbing between his toes.
Black cats have always brought good luck to me
They're the nicest cats that you'll ever see.
I like to give him kisses on his forehead
I give him kisses before we go to bed.
He likes to play around with some of his toys.
He's always quiet and he never makes noise
Except for when you brush his fur,
He likes it so much he starts to purr.
He was so tiny on the day that we found him
He was so small and he was really thin.
He's grown so much it's hard to believe he's the same cat.
He was so skinny now he's quite chunky and fat.
He likes to go outside and see all the birds.
I Love him so much it goes beyond words.

He's My Friend

Shadow sits by my side
As we stare at the sun,
He's my closest ally
He's Loved by everyone.
He's got gold eyes
And a cold wet nose,
He has fur between his toes.
He stares out the window
Looking for mice,
He thinks catching a rabbit
Would be quite nice.
He Loves me as much as I Love him
I Love him just like he's kin.
Soon he'll be sleeping and start to snore
He dreams of running outside the front door.
After a while he'll wake up and stare with his eyes
As he looks all around and stares up to the skies.

I Could Not Ask For More

You're the best friend I've ever had
When you're not around I feel so sad,
You're so sweet and you're so swell
If you're not here, life doesn't go well,
You're the nicest guy I know
When you're around things just flow,
You're the man that makes me smile
It's been that way now for a while,
You're the reason I keep on living
That's because of all the Love you're giving,
You're always going to be my man
I'll give you all the Love I can,
You're the man with the biggest heart
I fell for you right from the start,
You're a better man than all the rest
When it comes to Love you are the best,
You're so gentle and you're so kind
When you're not close, I lose my mind,
You're the one who took away my fears
I've been in Love with you for so many years,
You're nice, you're smart and oh, so clever
I will surely Love you forever,
You're the one that I Love so much
I just Love your gentle touch,
You are simply my greatest friend
It'll be that way until Tyme ends.

I Don't Know What To Do

Today's a day when I'm feeling blue
I'm just so sad I don't know what to do.
I look around at all of this snow
It takes my mood and makes it low.
Outside the weather is so very cold
It makes me feel like I'm so old.
I'm tired of being alone and sad
I feel so sad and often bad.
I feel sorry for animals who live in the cold
There are very few places for them to go.
The birds struggle to find some food
But being in the cold can't feel very good.
I'm sorry for the animals that are all alone
They struggle to stay alive and find a home.
I'm so glad I have a big black cat
He eats too much and now he's fat.
He keeps me company when no one else is around
He sleeps all day but with little sound.
When it turns to night he'll sleep on my bed
He'll listen to all the things I've said.
When it's Tyme, we'll both fall asleep
And we'll sleep together without making a peep.
Maybe tomorrow better weather will come by soon
And brighten the day for people and animals too.

I Hope I See You Again

Last night I felt down, and then I cried
I feel like a part of me has just died,
We used to be friends, you were like my brother
You meant so much to me, more than any other,
We went places together, we were so close
You're avoiding me now, it makes me feel morose,
I miss the friends that we had, they were so cool
We used to hang out in hours after school,
We went to high school together, we were more than friends
I just hope that this is not the way that this ends,
I wonder if you even think of me
Is this the way things have to be?
I've called you on the phone, but you don't take my calls
I still dream we're walking those high school halls,
I hope your wife is pretty and that your kids are nice
Just reliving these old memories is how I suffice,
We'd be friends forever is what you said
I hope I see you again before I am dead.

I Love you...not just some of the Tyme
We spend together, but all of the Tyme
We share during our days by each other's
Side.

I Love snuggling with you under a blanket
Or on the couch or under the covers on our
Bed. Just holding onto your hand means so
Very, very much to me.

I Love it when you take the Tyme and tell
Me just how much I mean to you, too. Simple
Things that you do for me mean so much and
It fills my heart with joy and happiness.

I Love when we get to go places together
Like going to a store or going out to dinner
And just get to spend Tyme with each other.

I Love to tell you just how much you mean
To me...Those simple three words, "I Love
You" never get to be tired of hearing me tell
You or you telling me.

I love you so very, very much. I never thought
I would ever find Love again in my lifeTyme.
Little did I know that you would become the
Most important part of my world that I have
Ever had or had the joy to share all of my Tyme
With. Thank you for just being the wonderful
Person that you are...You make life worth
Living!!

I Love You, I Do

Take a look in my eyes
I wear no disguise
All I can see is Love
Sent from heaven above.
So gently take my hand
It's Tyme to take a stand
Tell me your Love is true
I'll leave it up to you
We belong here together
We've withstood the weather
Now Take me in your arms
Your heart oh, how it warms
Hold me close to your heart
And let all of our Love now start
It will grow, it will expand
It will spread across the land
I've only one request of you
Tell me your Love is true
Tell me your Love is for me
And I will share mine with thee
Together we'll shine on through
I Love you, how I do.

I Miss Summer

I'm so tired of all this wintry mess
But in Winter that's the way that it gets.
I'm dreaming of all the things I miss in Summer
Because all of this snow is such a bummer.
I miss green grass and the leaves on the trees.
I miss going for walks in the breeze.
I miss the sun as she shines so bright.
I miss sleeping in a tent at night.
I miss swimming in a warm lake in June.
I miss laying in the sun on a warm afternoon.
I miss the songbirds as they fly around.
I miss the weather and all of it's sounds.
I miss the fireworks on the fourth of July.
I miss just watching the butterflies fly.
I miss watching the flowers as they bloom.
I miss watching the stars and the moon.
I miss watching the lawn as it grows.
I miss the feeling of sand in my toes.
I miss going camping outdoors.
I miss making some s'mores.
I miss watching the honeybees fly.
I miss watching the day pass slowly by.
I miss going for a walk in the rain.
I miss seeing the gulls and the cranes.
I miss seeing people enjoying the sun.
I miss seeing the sun set when the day is done.

I Think of You

All you ever do is think of you
Such a rotten thing for you to do.
You don't even bother to answer the phone
All you want to do is be alone.
The way you play the game of life is rude
Then you even have the nerve to ask for free food.
The way you treat our mom is like a pest
You never give her a chance to rest.
You're old enough to clean up your own house
You're really nothing more than just a louse.
All you ever do is take and never give
That's not the way your supposed to live.
You only invite mom over to help you clean
That's not the way life supposed to have been.
You can clean you house by getting off your bum
You need to depend upon yourself and not our mum.
You're not a kid you're fifty flour years old
And that's not the fist Tyme you've been told
I'm sick of the way you treat our mother
You need to do things on your own but never bother.
One day you'll be the end of her
You treat her like she's some old cur
Someday soon I hope you'll heed the words I've said
You'll have to care for yourself when she is dead.

If You Please

The sun is finally shining
The weather's going to change
It's Tyme to finally get going
It's Tyme to rearrange.
Little by little the grass is growing
The leaves are on the trees
Life is finally coming around
With all the birds and bees.
The temperature is rising
As some ducks go waddling by
They're off to take a swim
In a pond that's really close by they'll fly.
The sun's reflecting off the water
Some geese are taking a swim
When the weather's this nice
They want to jump right in.
If you stand right by the water
You can skip a stone
When the weather's just so good
You don't want to be alone.
Oh, yes the days are warming up
You can feel a gentle breeze
It's Tyme to have some fun
You'll find happiness if you please.

I'm here for you when things don't come out right
I'm here for you when you can't find the light.
I'm here for you when you're down and low
I'm here for you when you've got nowhere to go.
I'm here for you when people seem unkind
I'm here for you when no one seems to mind.
I'm here for you when your world seems upside down
I'm here for you when all you have is a frown.
I'm here for you when you're up and wired
I'm here for you when you're feeling tired.
I'm here for you when you need a hand to hold
I'm here for you when you're feeling cold.
I'm here for you when you're all alone
I'm here for you when you can't get anyone on the phone.
I'm here for you when you need a friend
I'm here for you when your heart needs to mend.
I'm here for you when you're feeling sad
I'm here for you when you feel really mad.
I'm here for you when you feel tattered and torn
I'm here for you when you feel you've been scorned.
I'm here for you when you need someone to talk with
I'm here for you when you need someone to walk with.
I'm here for you when you are feeling small
I'm here for you when you run into the wall.
I'm here for you when you aren't feeling proud
I'm here for you when the world seems too loud.
I'm here for you when you're feeling smug
I'm here for you when you need a hug.

Here I sit alone in Tyme
How I wish that you were mine.
We used to be such good friends
Why did it have to come to an end?
We used to have so much to say
But now that has all gone away.
Now all I do is sit and stare
I feel your presence in the air.
Little things remind me of us two
Oh, how I'm here just feeling so blue.
We were good friends when we were young
Oh, how we used to have such fun.
But you've passed on from this life
And I'm still crying in the night.
I think of all our Tyme together
And how we would have made it forever
Now you're in heaven looking down on me
I know you're an angel who lives in heaven so free.
I know we'll meet up on another plane
And our friendship will thrive again.
Until that Tyme I must hold on tight
Till we meet again in an ethereal light.

This world has become a gigantic mess
Too many problems I must confess.
Wherever you look things are going bad
I really must say it leaves me quite sad.
Too much of this, or too little of that
A crying shame is where it's at.
Watch what you say and watch what you do
Or they'll be pointing a finger at you.
This world has gone beyond politically correct
There's no more Love and there's no more respect.
Try to find beauty in the littlest of things
Try to find joy in the gifts that life brings.
Find your happiness in those that you Love
And find you peace in God above.

In Paradise

I just want you to know
You're a beautiful soul
You're sweet and so kind
You have a beautiful mind
You're brave and you're strong
In my life you belong
When I look in your eyes
I see paradise
You have a wonderful touch
I just Love you so much
You're the man of my dreams
Who helps hatch my schemes
You're simply the best
You make me feel blessed
You're my closest friend
I'll be with you till the end
You'll be forever in my heart
The two of us shall never part
I'm so glad you're with me
By your side I shall be
You have angel wings
You make my heart sing
You're humble and handsome
You took my heart ransom
We'll forever together be
Come spend eternity with me

SomeTymes life can be difficult its hard to face
It's hard to put my emotions in their place.
I get to the point where I just feel so low
I don't know how much lower I can go.
It's at these Tymes I need a good friend
Someone who can help my sad heart to mend.
SomeTymes I need to speak with someone on the phone
It makes it easier than to be all alone.
SomeTymes I need someone to lend an ear
It gets hard to find someone who wants to hear.
Life can be so hard when you feel down
SomeTymes I just get sick of living in this town.
SomeTymes it can help to put some music on
It's hard to focus when you're so far gone.
SomeTymes it feels like I'm so out of touch
Being around others can really help so much.
Life gets even harder when there's nasty weather
It's at these Tymes when we have to stick together
There are Tymes when it helps to spend Tyme with my cat
Because I'm really down that he helps me with that.
There are Tymes it helps me to go outside
And too it someTymes for me to go for a ride.
SomeTymes it's the best thing to just get some sun
Because when you're down it can help a ton

It Doesn't Get any Better Than This

It's nice to have friends like you
That share the wonderful things I do.
We've been friends for 28 years
I hold you in my heart so dear.
I relish the Tyme we spend together
We get together despite the weather.
We always have a really good Tyme
I'm so glad you're a friend of mine.
Often Tymes we go out to eat
Spending Tyme with you is a treat.
But we don't have to spend money to have fun
We can have a great Tyme just enjoying the sun.
SomeTymes we'll share a glass of wine
A bottle of wine makes everything fine.
We can have fun just going for a walk
While other Tymes we just sit and talk.
We have fun when we go to a store
It beats the heck out of being bored.
We can spend hours just listening to tunes
Or just enjoying the constellations and moon.
SomeTymes we just watch the cars go by
When we're together the Tyme just flies.
We end our Tyme together with a kiss
It doesn't get any better than this.

It Goes Beyond Sadness

SomeTymes I feel good and someTymes bad
A lot of the Tymes I feel really sad.
I don't like to feel this way
I wish my sadness would just go away.
I take my meds just like I should
I just wish they made me feel good.
SomeTymes they work someTymes they don 't
I don't like it when they won't.
SomeTymes it feels like a storm in my head
When I feel this way I wish I was dead.
I can't make the storm to stop
It seems I feel this way a lot.
It's very hard to live with depression
SomeTymes it leaves me full of aggression.
It isn't easy to live this way
It's the perfect way to ruin your day.
It's like drowning in water that's deep
When it gets really bad I just go to sleep.
This way of life it never ends
It helps me when I talk to my friends.
People say "I know how you feel,"
But living like this is so surreal.
In the depression game I'm just a pawn
I hope they find a cure before I'm gone.
People always ask why I never smile
They wouldn't if they walked in my shoes a while.

Shadow is busy giving himself a bath:
He starts with his ears
Than he moves to his paws,
When he's done washing his face
He carefully washes his whiskers, too.
Soon he moves on to his belly
Making sure he's gotten all of it clean.
After that he moves on to his back side
And tail including his back paws.
When he has finished cleaning himself
He sees that it is Tyme for another nap,
He puts his head down on his two front paws
Then he closes his eyes and goes back to sleep
For the third Tyme today.
It's a rough life having to go from
Nap to nap to nap…but someone's got to do it.
It might as well be him.

It's Getting Old

The snow is deep, the wind is cold
This Winter weather is getting old.
All I can do is think of spring
And get outside to do fun things.
This weather is great if you like to skate
But it's the weather like this I hate.
If you like you can do some sledding
Just think of all the pounds you'll be shedding
Some folks like to go outside to do some skiing
Just think of all the warm layers you'll be needing.
Then there's the snow that gets so deep
As Jack Frost will be there without a peep.
He makes the wind and wintry weather
So you'll need to stay warm by huddling together.
When you're done with the Tyme outside
Have some hot chocolate to warm you inside.
The kids enjoy making a snowman or two
It can be a fun thing for you to do.
Kids Love making a mountain of snow
They don't even care if it's cold.

It's Halloween

It's a good Tyme
To go trick or treating,
When we get back home
All our treats we'll be eating.
At a Halloween party
For apples we'll be bobbing
And a scary jack-o-lantern
We'll soon be a carving.
Inside of the pumpkin
We'll put a lit candle,
We'll then put it up
Way high on the mantle.
We'll go trick or treating
Wearing different faces,
We'll then go door to door
To many different places.
When we get back home
We'll be eating our candy,
From all of our treats
We'll be feeling so dandy.
So let's all enjoy
These last days of Fall,
It's truly the scariest
And best season of all.

It's Raining Again

It's raining again today
I know you must be on your way
It's too late for you to stay
All my skies have turned to gray
We'll meet again where angels play
Oh, God help me it's raining today.

It's raining again
I know I'm losing a friend
I try to stay calm and count to ten
I hope our paths will cross in the end
I'll let this Love help me to mend
Oh, help me God it's raining again.

It's raining once more
I see your shadow in the door
My tears form and fall to the floor
When it rains it will always pour
I hope our paths will cross once more
Oh, help me God it's raining once more.

It's raining outside
I have feelings I can't hide
It's going to be a bumpy ride
I can't understand, but I have tried
I tried to smile, but I just cried.
I feel like part of me has died.

It's Raining Again

The drops are slowly falling
Outside my window pane,
Everything is cold and wet,
No nothing stops the rain.
Everything is chilly and damp,
The weather's wet and cold,
It leaves me feeling weak
It leaves me feeling old.
I just don't like this weather,
This weather makes it hard to smile,
No, I don't like this weather
It's been that way for a while.
I look up in the air
The drops fall from the sky,
The sky is dark and ominous
It leaves me wondering just why.
I look so very high up
To see the sky is filled with clouds,
The lightening flashes on and on
The thunder crashes so loud.
I'm tired of being here indoors
I wish I could go outside and play,
I hope this rain is over soon
I'll just have to have fun another day.

Fall is now over
Winter is near
Snow is now falling
Not far from right here.
The flakes are all falling
They're as cold as ice
They tickle your face,
They feel chilly and nice.
They collect in piles
Upon the cold hard ground
They lay there quiet
Without any sound,
And when the wind blows
They fly through the air.
They feel nice and cold
On cheeks that are bare.
They say they're all different
No two are the same,
They'll be here on Christmas
When you call out Santa's name.
You can group them together
Into piles big and high,
Whenever they fall
From a cold winter sky.

It's the Perfect Day

It's the perfect day to spend with you
There's so many things that we could do,
We could sit in the shade down by the brook
Or watch a movie, let's take a look,
We could go to the beach and build castles of sand
Or listen to the music of our favorite bands,
We could sit side by side and make some wishes
Or go to the lake and catch some fishes,
We could go over to the nearest park
And swing until it gets really dark.
We could sell glasses of lemonade
Or sit on the grass by the tree in the shade,
We could go out to a restaurant and eat
Some great Thai food would be a treat,
We could go to the water park and get wet
Or stop by the casino and place a bet,
We could go to the ice rink for a skate
Or shop till we drop till it gets late,
Yes there are so many things we could do
When I get to spend my day here with you.

It's Tyme For Some Sun

It's Tyme for Some sun, so let it shine
It helps to make folks feel divine.
It helps the plants and trees to grow
It'll lift your spirits when you feel low.
It leaves shadows on the ground
It warms the earth without a sound.
It bathes the planet in its light
It turns the dark into the bright.
It makes the night turn into day
It gives us light so we can play.
It provides the earth with heat
It's warming power can't be beat.
It is really just one big star
It shines upon us from afar.
It brings about our four seasons
It rotates without any reason.
It makes water evaporate
It helps our Summers to be great.
It's the center of a solar eclipse
It's the center of our yearly trips.

Julie

You were the first Love in my life,
I thought that you would be my wife.
But Mother Nature had other plans,
Still we ended up being good friends.
We used to play out in the yard,
We used to play all day and hard.
I'm so glad that we're still friends,
You have helped my mind to mend.
All these years later we're still mud buddies,
When I look back it sure was funny.
Remember the pancakes your mother made?
It's a memory I could never trade.
You were so cute in your little dress,
And me in my sailor suit all nice and pressed.
We had fun like you'll never see in those days gone by,
If we'd had wings you know we'd have flied.
Oh, those wonderful days gone by,
Those wonderful days gone by,
Those wonderful days gone by.

Take a look at me and what do you see?
A man whose lost in the air that he breathes.
A man whose depressed and feeling down
A man who watches the world go round.
A world that's in chaos, a world gone bad
A place that makes its citizens feel sad.
And so he escapes in the music he hears
And tries to find solace in spite of his tears.
So he turns his head to heaven above
As he tries to find peace and tries to find Love.
No the world is not what it used to be
No longer a home to the land of the free.
It's now a place of murder and crime
It's now a place lost in sorrow and Tyme.
It's become a place that's harder to live
Where nobody cares and nobody gives.
Now it's a place where nobody shares
Now it's a place where nobody cares.
So raise your hands to heaven and pray
We can make it through another bad day.

Last Night

Late last night I had a dream
You came to me and then I screamed.
I dreamt that you were still alive
Even though I knew you had died.
I wasn't sure just what to say
And then I dreamed you walked away.
I woke up scared and full of fright
Until I saw the morning light.
Suddenly it all became clear
I was awake and full of fear.
I still remember the day you passed
I knew that you were gone at last.
I felt sad and yet relieved
You could no longer torture me.
I know you're gone, still I don't cry
Even though twelve years has gone by.
I remember when I was at your grave
It was so hard to still be brave.
I hadn't seen you in so long
The way I felt just seemed so wrong.
I felt guilty because I didn't feel sad
But those who knew you could understand.
You were never happy throughout your life
This made you miserable and full of strife.
I hope you're happy now wherever you are
And looking down from behind a star.

The sun is shining through my window
The sunlight warms the room,
Outside the world's getting warmer
The flowers are starting to bloom.
The grass is growing nicely
The grass is growing high,
Everywhere are signs of Spring
A butterfly floats on by.
Over there I see a squirrel
He's searching for some food
He's busy digging up the ground
He thinks the weather is good.
Life is teeming in a nearby pond
By the pond I see a frog
He's trying to catch some flies
He's sitting on a log.
By the pond I see some ducks
As they go swimming by
They're learning to stretch their wings
And they're learning how to fly.

The sun is shining, the sky is blue
There's just so much that I'd like to do.
We could go to the park and fly a kite
When the weather's good it seems so right.
We could go to the lake and take a swim
In my swimming suit I be swimming in
We could go to the library and check out some books
There are so many there, just take a look.
We might just go for a walk around the block
We could take a walk down to the dock.
We could find someone and play Frisbee
I'll fly it back to you when you send it to me.
If you'd like we can spend some Tyme at the zoo
We can see some animals if you're wanting to.
If you're bored we can go out for a drive
We'll say hello whenever we arrive.
Maybe we can spend some Tyme with the cat
We can give him some treats if you're up for that.
We could go for a ride out on our bikes
We can do that if you'd really like.
We could just sit outdoors and soak up some sun
Tanning in the sun can be so much fun .
Or if you like we could just stay at home
SomeTymes it's just nice to spend Tyme alone

Life Is Too Short

I sit here thinking of you today
There's so much that I want to say.
It's been 30 years that we've been friends
But it's in you that our friendship depends.
We haven't talked in oh, so long
To me this just sounds way too wrong.
We haven't seen you in 15 years
That's a lot of whisky and a lot of beers.
We can drink and carry on and have a good Tyme
I hope the libations can last all night.
We hope you'll come and see us soon
So we can party in the light of the moon
We'll be getting up and getting down
It will give you a smile where you had a frown.
Some of us will act a fool
And some of us will act too cool.
Maybe we could watch a movie or two
Or play some games if you so choose.
I hope we will see you again my friend
Because life's too short to come to an end.

Life is Blue Without Sue

I'm talking today to my friend Sue
She lifts me up when I feel blue.
We've been close good friends, for almost thirty years
We've shared some good Tymes, we've also shared some tears.
When we're together we always connect
We share a life that's made of our respect.
We're two lost souls that belong together
We'll make it through any type of weather.
She's a beauty to behold, she's definitely quite pretty
She is also smart and she's also quite witty.
When we're together she helps me fight my manic
When she's not around I go into a panic.
We'll always stay so close until our lives end
We'll always be closer than all my other friends.

You're my good Lover
You're my good friend
We'll be together
From now till the end.

Nothing can stop us
Northing at all
Not even if they
Stand ten feet tall.

Right from the moment
We too are just one
From the start of the day
Until it is done.

We too are close, yes
We're built on Love
From down here on earth
To the heavens above.

We work together
We fight the good fight
To stop what is wrong
And make it all right

Live every moment
Like it's your last
Say hello to the future
And goodbye to the past.

I lost a very good friend today. I feel so down
I don't know what to do. My friend moved on
To a better place. Now I know she's not in any
Pain anymore. It happens to our friends as they
Get older. We want to hold them but they must
Move on. When they leave us we feel so lost.
But Tyme is one thing we cannot change. It's
Forever moving forward without delay. Losing
A close friend is so painful. We spend our days
Reliving our moments when they were still with
Us. SomeTymes it's like we lost a part of your
Family. No matter how hard you try, you can
Still feel abandoned. We relive our moments
Looking at old photographs. You remember all
The things that they told us. We recall the way
They spoke and their perfume. SomeTymes it
Feels like they are still with us, even though
They are gone. They stay with us in your heart.
What hurts the most is we can no longer hold
Them. We wonder if they still think of us too.
It helps to give us peace to think that they do.

My Best Friend

Shadow you're my best friend
On you I do depend
We'll be together till the end.

You bring me up when I am blue
What a wonderful thing to do
I'm so glad that I have you.

I'm always happy when you're around
You turn my frown upside down
I feel like I'm off of the ground.

You are always so kind
To your soul I will always bind
I can't get you off of my mind.

You make my heart to glow
You lift me when I am low
I'm so glad I can let you know.

I've Loved you from the start
You're here down in my heart
We'll never be far apart.

You're the one I Love
You're as gentle as a dove
You've been sent from heaven above.

You'll always be my friend
On you I do depend
We'll be together till the end.

My Friend Britt

I like hanging with my friend Britt
She can cheer me up with her wonderful wit
Laughing and lifting my spirits too
She lifts me up when I feel blue
We enjoy listening to good music together
We always get along despite the weather
We enjoy just going to the store
Just having fun, we like to explore
We can have fun just watching a movie
Hanging with her is always quite groovy
She is so nice and always so kind
She always helps free my cluttered mind
She always has interesting things to say
We have fun when we get together and play
She helps lift me up when I feel sad
She's one of the best friends that I have
No, she is not a fair-weather friend
She'll be there until the end.

My Friend Shadow

My friend Shadow is one of the nicest cats I have
Ever known. He starts his day by snuggling up
Next to me. As he lays there I brush his fur and
Brush his face. He Loves all of the attention. After
A half hour of snuggling he gets up and goes over
To his cat bed. Here he begins to wash his paws.
First his front paws and then his back paws. He
Always cleans himself after we have spent Tyme
Together. I'm not sure but I don't think he likes
The smell of humans on him. After he licks all of
His paws, he gently washes his face. First he will
Wash his nose, then his forehead and finally his ears.
When he is finished with his face then he will start
To clean his chest and belly…after that he washes
His back and tail. Usually after giving himself a
Bath he is tired and he will put his head down on
The edge of his bed and take a nice long cat nap
Because he is all warn out. He will stay alert to
See what is going on while he is sleeping. Just
The right noise and he will wake up and start his
Wake up with a yawn. SomeTymes he will breathe
Heavy like he has asthma. Thay say some pets
Take on the characteristics of their owners. Could
It be he has asthma like me? If he isn't completely
Awake he will go back to his cat napping till he is
Completely awake and ready for the rest of his day.

My Good Friend

I'll make a wish upon a star
I wish you weren't away so far.
It's so hard when you're not around
You're one of the best friends I've found.
When we're together Tyme just flies
I'm amazed at how you're oh, so wise.
We like to go out to eat
Hanging with you is always a treat.
When we're together we share some wine
You're always nice and oh, so kind.
SomeTymes we just watch a movie
You're so hip and oh, so groovy.
When we're together we share some tunes
I hope we'll be together really soon.
It's always fun when you come for a stay
I hope you'll never go away.

My Sweet Thoughts of You

When I'm feeling down
And don't know what to do,
I just close my eyes
And I dream about you.
I dream of you, I dream of you
Oh, how I dream about you.
You come to me
In all of my dreams,
You come to help me
Hatch my schemes.
In all that I see,
In all that I do,
I keep in my mind
My sweet thoughts of you.
When I'm feeling down
And feeling blue,
I hold in my dreams
My sweet thoughts of you,
My sweet thoughts of you,
I hold in my heart
My sweet thoughts of you.

You take my hand and hold it tight
You hold onto me throughout the night.
When I'm down and feeling blue
You always know just what to do
When I'm down you lift me high
You're my one and only guy.
When I'm up and feeling manic
You help me when I start to panic.
When I'm up and way too wired
You work me out until I'm tired.
You take my hand and hold it tight
You take what's wrong and make it right.
When I'm down and feeling blue
You hold onto me steady and true.
When I'm up and feeling manic
You calm me down when I get frantic.
When I'm up and way too wired
You hold onto me till my energy expires.
You take my hand and hold it tight
You hold onto me throughout the night.
You hold onto me each and every night.
You hold onto me all day and all night.
You hold onto me each day and night.

Napping In the Sun

Shadow lays in the sun
Under a big, bright sky,
He thinks catching some mice
Would be fun tonight.

Slowly he walks over
And sits down next to me,
As we sit in the shadow
Of a big oak tree.

He has big gold eyes
That stare round and round
He sees everything
That moves on the ground.

After a while
He nibbles some grass
He snuggles with me
As the hours pass.

Later in the day
He falls fast asleep
Then he starts to snore
As he dreams so deep.

While he's sound asleep
He begins to now dream
That he's catching some prey
In an elaborate scheme.

And late in the day
We begin to grow tired
We've had enough of the sun
As the day has expired.

Nature Survives

The leaves are gone
The trees are bare
It's just so cold
In the Winter air.
There is no sun
The sky is gray
It's just another
Cold wintry day.
The animals all
Try to stay warm
Surviving the season
Staying free from harm.
It's never easy
To forage for food
When it's a contest
Of bad over good.
The ground is frozen
It's that Tyme of year
And how to survive
Is never quite clear.
To get their water
They must eat the snow
It's never easy
With so many months to go.
The only good thing
Is Spring's on the way
And nature survives
Yet another cold day.

Ocean View

I stand out on the edge so far
I stare into the deep blue sea,
The water is so nice and clear
Come take a swim with me.

And as I stand there all alone
I feel my feet in the sand,
The beach is so nice warm
It's such a joy to see this land.

As I look there I see some shells, too
As I look out to the ocean,
I see the water's reflection,
The waves move in a gentle motion.

When I look far out from here
In the water I see some fishes,
And then I pick up some rocks
I skip a stone and make some wishes.

I'm in awe of this beautiful view
I hope the ocean always looks this way,
I just Love the beauty of the sea
I will come back another day.

I'm all alone and feeling so blue
I'm wishing I could still hold you.
I wish I could still hold your hand
Tyme spent with you just feels so grand.
I feel so sad when you're not around
For you are nowhere to be found.
I can't wait to hold you again
Because we're so much more than friends.
I keep you steadfast in my heart
I wish we weren't so far apart.
No, I can't wait to see you again
I doesn't matter where you've been.
I just long to hold you close
Your smile keeps me from feeling morose.
Soon I'll be holding you in my arms
As you fill me up with your stately charms.
Soon we will be close once more
And I'll be knocking on your heart's door.

One Day Soon

It was a cold Spring day like today
On the day that I was born,
I'm feeling lost again
I'm feeling so forlorn.

I don't know just why
I must always feel at bay,
I'm tired so tired of feeling sad
I'm so tired of feeling this way.

I need to take my Psych meds
To help with my depression,
But they don't always help
It's a cold and dark life lesson.

And as my life seems to go
I get so tired of feeling down,
If you look upon my face
You'll see I wear a frown.

And as the days wear on
I will start to cry,
I wish wasn't here
I wish that I would die.

And as the days go on
My depression gets in full blown
I'm so tired and I'm so sad
I don't like to be alone.

It's hard to be Bipolar
My moods change like the weather,
I hope that one day soon
I'll start to feel much better.

Hey there sun I see you shining
You know you've got me smiling
I know it's not Summer yet
But it could be tomorrow I bet
I look at the trees the leaves are growing
I can see them in the wind just blowing
In the trees the birds are building nests
I know they're wearing their Sunday best
They take Tyme feeding their young birds
And speak to them in chirpy type words
I see the squirrels looking for food
Searching for food puts them in a good mood
Hey the lawn is growing green
It's the nicest that I've seen
See that rabbit, his hunger has grown
He's hoping to find some food of his own
See the butterflies in the air
They fly through the air without any care
Hear the kids as they play with their friends
They hope that today never comes to an end
And when tonight as the sun sets in the west
You'll know today was one of your best.

The Other Side

The world is now spinning so fast and quite wrong
It's no longer a place where we all get along.
It's a world that's filled with sorrow and pain
It's a place where there's very little to gain.
So we feel full of sorrow and anger and rage
It's like we're trapped and locked in a cage.
SomeTymes it feels like nobody cares
It often feels like nobody shares.
We hang on tight to our faith and Love
We hang on even tighter to God up above.
We hope that he hears our voices here below
As we hang on tight to the things that we know.
And in the moments where life is too strange
We hope he'll help us to heal and to change.
So we can get to heaven and get our wings
And join in the choir where the angels sing.
So we try really hard to do our best
And change our world from east to west.
So we become a world of Love and pride
And hope for the best on the other side.

Our Beautiful Future

Here I sit alone and sad
Oh, how I'm just feeling so bad.
I sit here wishing you were here
And how I could still hold you my dear.
I wish I could hold you so tight,
And hold you till the Tyme is right.
Till then I'll hold you in my heart
And hope that we shall never part.
I long to hold you nice and close
To help me from feeling morose.
You lift me up when I feel down
You lift me higher when I frown.
Oh, how I long to hold your hand
When I'm with you life feels so grand.
Spending Tyme with you is nice
No one but you could ever suffice
So come and spend some Tyme with me
Our beautiful future is meant to be.

It's supposed to snow today again
And all I can do is pray for rain.
No more snow, please go away
I want the sun to shine today.
It's been cold for oh, so long
All this cold just feels so wrong.
I want to see leaves up in the trees
I want the grass to grow for me.
All this snow makes me want to scream
I want to wake up from this wintry dream.
So I begin to pray for rain
And I wish to see the sun again.
This Winter has been oh, so long
All this Winter just feels so wrong.
I want to see green leaves on the trees
I want the grass to grow for me.
This Winter weather makes me want to scream
Someone wake me from this long Winter dream.

Ray

He was a really close friend of mine
When we'd hang out we'd have a good Tyme.
He was handsome, tall and slim
But things weren't going so well for him.
I didn't know things had gotten so bad
Maybe I could have changed things if I had.
He blew his mind out in his car
His suicide's left me with a scar.
I wonder if I could have saved his life
After all these years I'm still filled with strife.
He was such a wonderful friend
We were close right till the end.
I didn't get to say goodbye
I wish I knew the reason why.
It's still hard for us to understand
You have to do the best you can.
Now he's an angel in the sky
And we're just left to wonder why.
If things start to go astray
You need to get help right away.
So keep your faith in God above
And shower the ones you have with love.

Sadness

Sadness flows like a river of rain
So much to lose, too little to gain.
I dim the lights and sit alone in the dark
This bit of sadness has left its mark.
I dream of things to make me feel better
I try so hard just to keep it together.
My mood changes from bright to black
I'm at the point of no turning back.
I feel like I'm all alone
It feels like my heart is blown.
I reach out to touch a heart that's broken
So I try to speak, but nothing is spoken.
SomeTymes it's like I'm dead inside
I feel so sad and I start to cry.
SomeTymes music can help a lot
Just the right song can hit the right spot.
Talking to a friend can help you out
It's so hard not to scream and shout.
When you're alone sadness can take its toll
Try to make recovering from sadness your goal.

There's a storm raging inside my head
It leaves me wishing I was dead.
I'm feeling down and feeling out
It makes me want to scream and shout.
I want this episode to be over
I don't think I can go much lower.
I just want to be feeling better
But my moods keep changing like the weather.
One day up, the next day down
On my face I wear a frown.
Maybe I'll feel better tomorrow
I'm so tired of all this sorrow.
So I call my friends up on the phone
But no one seems to be at home.
So I must face this depression by myself
And pull some smiles down from the shelf
For it's up there that I keep my feelings
I want to send this depression reeling.
But it just won't leave me so fast
I hope these feelings just won't last.
So I say my prayers to God above
And hope he'll send me down some Love.

Shadow

Shadow used to be my little black cat
He used to be quite skinny, now he's kind of fat.
He sleeps in his bed by the living room door
He likes his treats and always asks for more.
I can honestly say he's one of my best friends
It will be that way till the day his life ends.
And when he sleeps he snores quite loud
When he gives me kisses, it makes me feel quite proud.
He has beautiful eyes that shine just like gold
He comes when I call him, he does as he is told.
When he is in the basement, he likes chasing mice
He never acts mean, he always acts so nice.
He likes chasing squirrels, he likes chasing frogs
Instead of a cat, he acts more like a dog.
He has sharp white teeth, and a cold wet nose
He has lots of fur between all of his toes.
He always behaves, he never is a pest
Of all the pets I've had, he truly is the best.

Shadow 2

I Love my Shadow, yes I do
I know that he Loves me too
He's the cat that makes me smile
It's been that way now for a while.

He's the best cat I've ever had
Snuggling with him makes me feel glad
He loves stalking through the house
SomeTymes he'll even catch a mouse.

He loves running here and there
He likes napping everywhere
He sleeps all day and runs all night
SomeTymes he'll nip but never bite.

He cheers me up when I feel down
He'll always chase away my frown
He's the nicest cat I know
His fur shines with a bright glow.

When I pet him he'll always purr
He likes it when I brush his fur
His nose is wet and always cold
He has eyes that shine like gold.

When he's happy he'll wag his tail
At night we snuggle without fail
SomeTymes he likes a bit of cat nip
He's as sharp as any whip.

Shadow the Cat

He curls up in his warm, soft bed
He understands the words I've said.
He's my cat and I Love him so
I give him kisses on his nose.
His fur is short and shiny and black
He Loves it when I brush his back.
He meows when he's asleep
I wonder what he dreams so deep.
His eyes shine like they're made of gold
He cuddles with me when it gets cold.
His nose is dark and always wet
I couldn't ask for a nicer pet.
When he's tired he'll breathe a long sigh
He snuggles with me throughout the night.
He Loves to sit in the Summer sun
He thinks catching mice is fun.
He naps on and off throughout the day
He always thinks that it's Tyme to play.
He's not just a pet, he's my best friend
I know he'll be with me till the end.
He has pointed, shiny ears
Though he's asleep he still hears.
I wonder just what's on his mind
He's someTymes shy, but always kind.
When I pet him he just purrs
He's way cooler than a cur.
I Love him he's my shadow-bear
He's the one for whom I care.

Richard is so handsome
Yet he's as gentle as a dove,
I like spending Tyme with him
He's the one I Love,
He is so very nice
He is so very kind,
There's no one else I notice
There's no better man I'll find.
We spend Tyme together
We are so very close,
He's the one I so enjoy,
He's the one I Love the most.
We do lots of things together
We always have such fun,
I'll spend my whole life with him
Till all my days are done

It was a beautiful day in Summer
Staying inside would have been a bummer.
I went out walking for a while
The sun was shining so I cracked a smile.
I decided to get something good to eat
Some good Thai food would be a treat.
I went to my favorite restaurant, but it was closed,
It was because of Covid 19 I suppose.
So then I stopped and bought some lemonade,
It was so nice to drink it in the shade.
I called my friend Carol and said, "Lets go for a drive,
It's such a great day just to be alive."
We went for a walk down by the lake
It got so hot it was too much to take.
We got back in her car and just drove around,
We listened to Miles Davis, it was the perfect sound.
We listened to some good jazz music on a hot, hot day.
We felt like some kids who were at play.
We drove around till the sun started setting,
Tomorrow will be just as good day I'm betting.
It'll be another good day to soak up the sun,
Spending Tyme with friends is always fun.

Sue

Soon I'll be hanging with my friend Sue
She lifts me up when I feel blue.
When we're together, we always have fun
If I am the earth, then she is the sun.
I Love her because she's my soul sister
When she's not around I really miss her.
I miss her more than all of my friends
She is my oxygen, on her I depend.
I Love her more than I can express
When she's not around, my life is a mess.
I Love her so much, it's quite ethereal
When she's not around my life is surreal.
When she's not around, my life's without laughter
Wherever she goes I will follow right after.
She's my soul sister and I'm her soul brother
She lifts me higher than anyone other.
If she is my trainer, then I am her pet
Quite simply put, she's as good as it gets.

Summer's finally here
The grass is growing high
People are busy catching rays
As some insects fly on by.
People are outside working in the yard
Beneath the sky so blue
In the sun they start to tan
A breeze goes blowing on through.
By the lake some people are catching fish
And they're camping in a tent
People Love the warm weather
On a day that's heaven sent.
At a nearby park kids are swimming
They splash the water around
They enjoy their Summer break
The sounds of Summer abound.
In the sky I see a flock of birds
They're busy building their nests
They're teaching their young to fly
Summer really is the best.

Thank You For Just Being You

You're so kind
You're so special
You're just so cool
It blows my mind.

You can take an average day
And make it oh, so special
I'm thankful to you
For making my day today .

It's something you do so well
So thank you oh, my dear
Just for being here
And making my day so swell.

I hope that in my mind
I can do the same
You make me feel better
Just by being kind.

I hope you'll find
That I'm a good friend
It'll be that way till the end
Thank you for just being so kind.

That's the Way It Goes

It's a cool fall afternoon
The leaves are falling from the trees,
I feel them crunch beneath my feet
I hear them rustle in the breeze.

As I look up through the air
The sky is cloudy and gray,
The day is mellow and quite cool
It's just another autumn day.

And later on today
I'll look up and see the moon,
The air begins to chill
I know Winter will be here soon.

In not too many days
It will be Thanksgiving,
I'm glad for all I have
And all of life is giving.

Not too long from now
The air will be crisp and cold,
You'll feel it all around
It'll chill you to the bone.

And shortly in the future
The ground will be covered up in snow,
Winter's on its way here
That's just the way the seasons go.

The Beach

The waves are blue and so is the sky
The sight of the beach makes me feel so high.

The view of the shore puts my mind as ease
The sound of the water fills my heart with peace.

The sand of the beach gets between my toes
The smell of salt entices my nose.

The seagulls fly across the coastline
The turtles mosey around the shoreline.

The sunset on the beach is beautiful to behold
The color of the sand is a wonderful gold.

The crashing of the waves is relaxing to the senses
The length of the shoreline is without fences.

The edge of the ocean is encrusted with shells
The dolphins make sounds of chiding in spells.

The palm trees are scattered along the sandy shore
The coral grows along the beaches floor.

Starfish float along the beaches
The edge of the ocean is without reaches.

The Best of Friends

SpomeTymes it's like we are the best of friends
We'll stick together until the very end.
I tell you things that I can only tell you
You're the only one I can trust them to.
You tell me stories that are so profound
SomeTymes they can even shake the ground.
It's at these Tymes we have to stick together
And be like we're just two birds of the same feather.
Then there are those Tymes when you don't call
I can't get anyone on the phone at all.
You get upset by something that I said
So you end up not talking to me instead.
I don't like it when you act in this way
You don't listen to anything that I have to say.
You just shut down and cut me off
When were not getting along be so rough.
For now until we talk again someTyme later
Start acting like my friend and not a hater.

The Changing of the Seasons

The sun is shining
The clouds are flowing,
And the warm wind
Is gently blowing
The leaves are turning
And they are falling,
And as I walk
I hear you calling.
Outside the seasons change
From fall to winter,
We burn all the leaves
In a fire of cinder.
As day turns to night
The light glows dimmer
And in the sky
The stars now shimmer,
And in the dark
So shines the moon
And after the night
The day comes so soon.
With the end of fall
The new seasons take hold
It will soon snow
As the weather grows cold.
So soon comes the holidays
We'll decorate the tree
With shades of red and green
And I'll give gifts from you to me.
So come here soon
Let's enjoy each day
Enjoying Mother Nature
In every possible way.

The Color of Spring

I look out and see the lawn
The grass is slowly growing,
If the weather stays this way
The lawn I'll soon be mowing.
I look high up into the trees
I see all the shades of green,
Now the trees are full of leaves
It's just the way this Spring has been.
As I look up into the branches
I see the animals are out to play,
They all look so very cute
It takes my breath away.
Now it's slowly raining
The sky is filled with clouds,
I see the lightning flash
The thunder is so loud.
The day is very typical
For a day that is in Spring,
I'm glad for Mother Nature
And all the joy to us she brings.

He sits alone in a great big chair
But his mind is so very far from there.
He remembers when he went to school
The place he learned the Golden Rule.
He used to have so many friends
Thinking how they would be there till the end.
He recalls when his family was still together
He thought they'd make it through bad Tymes forever.
He remembers his very first Love
The kind of Love people only dream of.
He remembers his very first kiss
And how it filled his heart with bliss.
He remembers the day he lost his dad
The day he felt lost and so very sad.
He remembers the closeness he had with his brothers
Recalling the days when they were so much younger.
Now they get together on special days
But still they seem so far away.
Now and then he still thinks of them aloud
Even though they hang with a different crowd.
The Love of his family fills his heart
It's the kind of closeness you can't tear apart

The Evening Sky

There's a light up in the stars tonight
The way they shine up in the sky so bright.
The stars twinkle in the background of the sky so blue,
They twinkle in the backdrop of the evening so new.
Later I can see them twinkle in the dark evening breeze
When I can see them reflected in the water of the seas.
I watch them shine as I walk along in the land
I watch them as I walk along in the sand.
When I look up I see the constellations way up there
They move with the clouds blowing up in the air.
I look up and see the reflection of the moon
I know that the night will be ending quite soon.
I wish I could get up off of the ground
So that I could take one last look around.
I can now see the rising of the bright day's sun
A beautiful day has now just begun,
And as the night slowly begins to fade away
I see the dawning of a brand new day.

I look up to see the gardens of the sun
As I see that a new day's just begun.
I see the sun to rise up into the sky
Throughout the day the sun drifts on by.
And off of the water the sun escapes
Reflected in the beauty of all the landscapes.
The sun shines on through in the clouds as they blow,
The sun helps everything to live and to grow.
The sun shines on as the light flows on through
The sun shines on in the sky that's so blue.
The sun always shines with such great mirth
The sun always helps to warm up the earth.
The sun is big and yellow and round
The sun always shines on without any sound.
The sun flows like a river of light
The sun shines on from the morning till night.
The passing of the sun helps us make our days
The sun shines on with it's beautiful rays.
The sun sets at the beginning of the night
The sun shines as it gives us our light.
When the sun sets up comes the moon
The sun helps all of the world to bloom.

The Hottest Summer Ever

The sun shines down in a brutal heat
I feel so hot, I just feel so beat,
Everywhere you kook rays are burning down
It's hard to stay cool in this heat filled town,
I look for some shade, but there's none to be found
The hot rays are everywhere, they burn without sound,
The leaves are lifeless the grass is wilting, too
It's hard to stay focused when you're burning blue,
I'd go for a walk, but it's just too hot
I'll have some lemonade, it'll hit the spot,
I'm praying for rain to help me stay cool
It's a perfect day to swim in a pool,
The sun is casting shadows all over the place
I wish I lived in a much cooler space,
The sky is bright blue, not a cloud anywhere
You can feel the humidity in the molten air,
I need to wear a hat to keep the sun from my eyes
If you crack an egg on the ground, it'll fry,
You need to drink lots and lots of cool water
Just to keep from getting much hotter,
When night finally comes, you'll be so glad
This is one of the hottest Summers we've had.

Today we celebrate the joy of Love,
A gift God sent to the earth from above.
It's a feeling two people can share,
It's a way to show that they really care.
It happens when we put two hearts together,
It is a way their feelings can be measured.
It's a way they can express their bliss,
It all begins with the touch of a kiss.
It happens when their bodies become entwined,
It is a way they feel that comes from the divine.
It is a feeling they share when their bodies are united,
It is an emotion that they feel that can't be divided.
It is a feeling that can last forever and ever,
It is an emotion that they can forever endeavor.
Love is celebrated by the union of marriage,
Love is ended when the two become disparaged.
Love is celebrated with the wearing of rings,
Love is expressed when two hearts truly sing.
Love is strong and never ever ending,
Love is the result of two hearts truly expanding.
Love is the consequence of the union of souls,
Always remember to make Love your goal.

The Joy of Spring

When the snow is deep
And the air is cold
I can't help feeling
So very old and tired
I yearn for the weather of Spring
To make me feel young again
When the warm rays of sun
Make all the world anew
When all the earth is fresh
With the greens of flowers
Growing all over in every direction
Providing us with beauty
And helping us feel new
With the joy of Spring
And as we are entwined with it's sound
Of bees buzzing and butterflies flying
Wherever the eyes do roam
And as far as they can see
Leaving those dismal days
Of Winter far behind
And the world all aglow
With the life and joy of youth
Watching life flourish
And be renewed with
The beauty of the sun's return
To claim her thrown
As the bringer of all that lives alive
Here's to the joy of Spring
And here's to the beauty of the sun.

In search of you
I found myself,
I saw me perching
On a shelf.
Then around myself
I did unfold,
And this a heart
That's made of gold.
I've been lucky
I know it's true,
I have good memories
Of me and you.
In all that I see
And all that I do,
I keep in my mind
These sweet thoughts of you.
When I'm so down
And feeling bad,
I just reflect
On the Love I've had.

He sits alone in a great big chair
But his mind is far from there.
He thinks back to when he was young
And all the songs that he had sung.
He remembers when he had so many friends
The ones he thought would be there till the end.
He thinks back to all the lessons he had learned
The kind to keep him from getting burned.
He remembers his very first Love
The kind that people only dream of.
He remembers his Love for his mom and dad
The kind of Love that they can no longer have.
He misses the Tymes his family was still together
He thought that they would stay close forever.
He misses the Love he had for his brothers
Remembering when they were much younger.
He thinks of how they played so much
Now they seem so far out of touch.
He longs to be young one more Tyme
And recall all of his nursery rhymes.
He wants to live his life once more
Reliving the moments he so Loved for sure

The Other Side

The world is now spinning so fast and quite wrong
It's no longer a place where we all get along.
It's a world that's filled with sorrow and pain
It's a place where there's very little to gain.
So we feel full of sorrow and anger and rage
It's like we're trapped and locked in a cage.
SomeTymes it feels like nobody cares
It often feels like nobody shares.
We hang on tight to our faith and Love
We hang on even tighter to God up above.
We hope that he hears our voices here below
As we hang on tight to the things that we know.
And in the moments where life is too strange
We hope he'll help us to heal and to change.
So we can get to heaven and get our wings
And join in the choir where the angels sing.
So we try really hard to do our best
And change our world from east to west.
So we become a world of Love and pride
And hope for the best on the other side.

The perfect Night

I look into your eyes
And I see my reflection there
In your eyes you smile
It shows me that you care

You tell me that you Love me
Indeed I know it's true
And my Love is returned
When I hold onto you.

Late when we are sitting
I hold onto your hand
You squeeze my hand so gently
You're such a gentle man.

Then you pull me close to you
Then I can taste your lips
Your mouth is close to mine
Now I can get your kiss.

Slowly you pull me closer
Then you take off your clothes
Then I take off of mine
That's just the way it goes.

When I'm in your arms
You hold onto me tight
Then you kiss me and Love me
It's an end to the perfect night.

The Sound of Silence

As I step into the nightTyme shadows
I listen to the world all around me.
I hear the sound of some crickets chirping
And the sound of some frogs croaking.
In the distance I hear the sound of some cars driving by.
And in the mix of it I hear the sound of the wind in the trees.
When it's dark you can really notice the sounds that you
Take for granted in the daylight when all is buzzing by you.
All of everything is peaceful in the night.
You can even notice the sound of the footsteps you are making.
The beauty of the stars lights your path in the moon's shadow.
If you look long enough you may even see a shooting star.
I Love going for a walk in the nightTyme because the hurried
Pace of the world slows down and everything is so placid.
At night everything is more calm and peaceable.
Something that is in such a busy place as our hurried world
Moves by more slowly and at a pace that is a joy to see and hear.
Oh, what a beautiful thing to behold…The sound of silence.

It was the usual Saturday night growing up
The stereo was so loud the speakers were
Buzzing and sounding distorted, but that
Didn't change anything… my father was
In one of his moods when he wanted to
Listen to his music. This was fueled by an
Entire day and evening of hard drinking
Some whiskey and Seven, and lots and
Lots of beer. On the floor all scattered all
Throughout the room were his L.P.s. He
Was looking at all of the records and he
Was deciding which ones he had played
And was now deciding which ones to play
Next. Then he moved around the room
And he picked one up and walked back
Over to the stereo and proceeded to place
It so it would be the next to play. Then he
Turned the knob so it would play. Then
Loudly over the crackling speakers began
To blurt out Release Me by Englebert
Humperdinck. This was all he needed to
Inspire him to start singing along…and he
Did…and he did…and he did, so he did
Till we began to tune out his singing because
He was singing off key. The speakers
Crackled with the sound of the record
Sounding distorted. Then he picked up his
Hands out in front of himself and he began
To conduct the instruments that were playing
On the recording. He began to sing and wave
His hands back and forth and started to sing
Along with Englebert until that side of the
Recording finished playing. Then he walked
Over and picked up another record and so it
Began again all over again…and a one…and
A two…and a three…

The Very Best Season

The leaves are falling
From all of the trees,
We hear them crunch
In a cool Fall breeze.
The clouds now form
Into a big wisp,
The air chills our cheeks
When the air is so crisp.
Up in the heavens
The skies turn to gray,
The sky won't be blue
For many a day.
We'll carve us a pumpkin
Into a Halloween dream,
Kids dressed up as ghouls
Will make us all scream.
On a cold dark night
They'll go trick or treating
When they get back home
All their candy they'll be eating
So now let's now enjoy
The last days of Fall
It's such a great season
It's the best of them all.

They've Left Their Mark

I hear voices in my head
They make me wish that I was dead.
I hear voices in my mind
The things they say are so unkind.
I don't like the things they say
I wish they would just go away.
I don't like the things I hear
They fill my mind with dread and drear.
I hear voices when I'm alone
They say things that chill me to the bone.
I hear voices in my ear
They make me wish I wasn't here.
I hear voices in my room
They fill my heart with dread and doom
I hear voices all around
I don't like the way they sound
I hear voices when I'm in the dark
On my mind they've left their mark.

As I go through this life, I live it full of sadness
Often feeling down and often full of madness.
Being crazy isn't easy, it's often full of hell
It surely isn't easy living life in a shell.
It's a shell of what was once the former me
Just a little fragment of who I used to be.
When I get really low I talk to my friends
We often talk till the sadness ends.
Still there are days nothing seems to fix it
I get really down and nothing seems to nix it.
I get so really down and low all I can do is to cry
And no matter what I do nothing dries my eyes.
As I live my life my color changes to blue
And I just don't know why, I haven't got a clue.
So I say my prayers and pray to God up above
I hope that he'll hear me and send me some Love.
Until I get to heaven where everything's fine
I hope he'll look down and share some Love divine.
But nothing's for certain, so I just sit here and groan
I try to live the best that I can, and fight this one alone.

This Crazy World

This world is crazy and it makes me sad
It's hard to believe things have gotten so bad,
Dirty water and polluted air
It sure fills me with despair,
Distorted truth and hate filled lies
There's just do much you can despise,
Hunger here and sickness there too
It's hard to wonder what to do,
Our empire has risen and now it will fall
It's getting hard to cope with it all,
Our world has become a colossal mess
It's hard to have faith I must confess,
Be kind to those you come across
And hope your life's not a total loss
Don't believe everything you read
And say a prayer for those in need,
Find strength in those that you Love
And try to find faith in God above.

This Life in the Blues

Yesterday's gone and tomorrow's soon to follow
And everything I do leaves me feeling so hollow.
So I try to fight this depression and all of this sadness
Still I feel so empty and often full of madness.
Look up to the sky, it's full of shades of gray
So I just hope there'll be a sunny kind of day.
I long to hold you close, and dry away my teary eyes
I wonder if I'll ever find some real happiness inside.
When you're close to me I lose myself in a song
Funny when you're here we always get along.
I Love the way you make me feel safe and all's right
And when you're in my arms I want to hold you real tight.
I wish I could make things all right for you
I only wish that you feel the same way too.
We have depended on each other to get through this strife
It's not the way it's supposed to be in this game of life.
One day our future will come to a bitter end
When we get to heaven we'll still be friends.
Until that Tyme comes around I pray for me and you
And we'll have to live this life in the blues.

Till Morning Creeps

I look deep into your eyes
And I feel Love as no surprise,

I reach down and hold your hand
My feelings lost at your command,

Then you wrap yourself around me
As feelings of Love now surround thee,

Now I tilt my head and give you a kiss
I am now lost in a state of total bliss,

I feel my heart now beating fast
It's good to feel Love in total at last,

Then we hug and kiss some more
I am now lost at heaven's door,

Making Love to you just feels so good
It feels just like I knew it would,

Now we collapse and fall asleep
As we stay wrapped till morning creeps.

Till the End

He lays there softly snoring
As he sleeps in his little bed,
He's dreaming of eating cat nip
While dreams circle in his head.
As I look upon him
His fur is soft and dark,
I'm thinking of taking him outside
Maybe I'll take him to the park.
If I take him outside
He'll go searching for some prey,
Like rabbits and some squirrels
To chase around on a cool Fall day.
He likes taking cat naps
Of all things he likes best is to sleep,
And searching for some mice
In the basement dark and deep.
When he's curious his tail will wag
Its made of soft black fur
He always seems so happy,
And when he is he softly purrs.
I so enjoy spending Tyme with him
I'm so glad he is my friend,
We enjoy our Tyme together
I'll Love till the end.

I love you
You're my friend
Until the end.
I Love you
You're so kind
It blows my mind.
Thank you for being my friend
I will Love you till the end
I will Love you until the end.
I Love you
You're my friend
Until the end.
I Love you
You're so sweet
Being with you is such a treat.
I Love you, yes I Love you
I will Love you till the end
So I thank you
Yes, I thank you
I thank you for being my friend
I will Love you
Yes, I will Love you
I will Love you till the end.

Together Until the End

Today's the perfect day to spend with you,
There's nothing more that I'd rather do.
I lay here with you, right here next to me,
There's so many things to do and to see.
So I spend my Tyme here with my cat
His eyes are gold and his fur is black.
His name is Shadow and he's my closest friend
And we'll be together until the end.
We like to sit on the porch and watch the birds
We talk with each other without the need for words.
We communicate with just our smile
It's been that way now for a while.
I really enjoy when we nap together
It's something we can do despite the weather.
He likes to sleep curled up in a little ball
We nap whether it's Winter, Spring, Summer or Fall.
When he takes a nap he snores just a bit
This is as good as life can get.

There are those days you have when nothing
Goes right, despite your wishes to change them.
This has been one of those weeks where every
Thing has gone wrong and the week is just
Crawling by at a snail's pace. I just wish that
Was over. Unfortunately you can't speed up
Tyme so you must just endure it and hope for
It to be over soon. I wish I could just make all
My sadness go away. I have been feeling so
Depressed I don't know what to do to get on
Through this. When you're feeling sad and
Blue you get tired so easy. Your body aches
And nothing feels right. All you can do is try
To keep your head above water and try not to
Let everything get to you. This is obviously
Easier said than done. When you suffer from
Bipolar depression, the feelings of sadness
Can come at you like waves that push you
Under and drag you down to the depths of
Sadness and worry like you've never seen
Before. When you get this down it can be
Very hard for you to keep going and continue
On with your life. SomeTymes the sadness
Is so overwhelming you get to the point to
Where you think that suicide is the only way
Out. It is than that you must reach out to other
People and seek to see if a therapist to help
You through these difficult Tymes. It's okay
To say I need help right now and do whatever
You need to keep on going. Don't give up
Because these feelings will pass and you can
And will feel better eventually.

I'm feeling low and feeling bad
I'm so tired of feeling sad.
I'm so sad it makes me cry
It makes me wish that I would die.
I'm tired of living in my head
I often wish that I was dead.
I'm feeling down and feeling blue
I wish I knew just what to do.
I wish I felt like I fit in
I'm sick of living in this skin.
I feel like I'm flying blind
I know my future doesn't look so kind.
It's so hard to keep on going
I know my weakened mind is showing.
I turn to God and then I pray
I'll make it through another day.
I hope that I will somehow mend
I'll take my meds until the end.

Valentines Day

Today is the day we celebrate the joy of Love,
A gift Gad made to the earth from above.
Love is a feeling two people can share,
Love is the feeling that shows that they care.
Love is the result of two hearts joining together,
Love is the way these feelings can be measured.
Love is the way that two can share their bliss,
Love is shared with the joy of a kiss.
Love is the result of two bodies entwined,
Love is a gift that is truly divine.
Love is the way two bodies are united,
Love is a feeling that can't be divided.
Love is a feeling that can last forever,
Love is made when two hearts do endeavor.
Love is celebrated by the wearing of rings,
Love is expressed when two hearts truly sing.
Love is made from the hearts truly expanding,
Love is forever and never ever ending.
Love is the result of the union of souls,
Always remember to make Love your goal.

When I go for a walk tonight
I'll be holding your hand so tight.
We'll be gazing at the stars
And staring at the moon and Mars.
We'll go for a walk down by the park
There we'll stay till it gets dark
So we'll sit and have a swing
And talk about the state of things.
We will talk about the weather
As we sit and swing together.
We'll go for a trip down on the slide
Then on the merry-go-round we'll ride.
Then we'll walk down by the lake
And skip some stones and some wishes we'll make
We can see all of the wildlife there
In the moonlight that shines everywhere.
We'll stop and feed the ducks some food
And watch them swimming with their brood.
We'll sit and talk for a good long while
Then we'll stroll home, about a mile.
And as we make it to the door
We'll stop and think of tomorrow some more
And the walk that we'll be taking then
Oh, what a beautiful night it's been.

What I'm Feeling

I'm feeling down and I feel sad
I don't know why I feel so bad
This crazy world just makes me mad
I think it's the good luck I've never had.

I'm feeling down and I'm feeling out
I just want to scream and shout
It's all this chaos that's about
All this negativity fills me with doubt.

I'm feeling down and feeling cursed
I feel like I'm going to burst
My emotions are taught and my lips are pursed
I don't think I've ever felt any worse.

I'm feeling down and I just cried
I have a lot of hurt inside
I feel like part of me has died
My feelings stem from a lack of pride.

I'm feeling down and I feel sore
I'm feeling rotten to the core
When it rains it always pours
I can't hide my feelings anymore.

I'm feeling down today
I wish I didn't feel this way
There's not much left for me to say
We all die in the end anyway.

When I Feel Blue

You bring me up when I feel blue
What a nice thing for you to do
You calm me down when I am mad
You always leave me feeling glad
I like it when we take a walk
When we do we like to talk
About the state of the world we're in
And where we've gone and where we've been
When I'm down and when I cry
You always help me dry my eyes
You cheer me up with a smile on your face
You help me to keep my thoughts in place
I'm so glad that you're my friend
You've helped my broken heart to mend
You make me feel like I could sing
And that is a truly wonderful thing
And when I've fallen into a pit
You always help me out of it.

When I'm With You

When I'm with you, Tyme stands still and I am
Lost in moments of joy and happiness.

When I'm with you, nothing else matters and I
Am I am so glad for the Tymes we get together.

When I'm with you, I am reminded just how
Special and thoughtful you are. These are the
Moments that I treasure most, these moments
We share together.

When I'm with you I feel free to just be me
And not have to prove anything to anybody.

When I'm with you Tyme stands still and I get
Caught up in the moments where I am just
Sharing my Tyme with you.

When I'm with you I know heaven exists as I
Am in heaven whenever you are near me, it is
A feeling that cannot be ignored.

When I'm with you I enjoy each and every
Minute we share together. Each and every
Second counts and matters, and I look forward
To spending them all with you.

When I'm with you I know that Love is the only
Emotion that matters and it means the universe to
Me...You are my whole universe and so much
More than I can ever tell you.

Outside the sun is shining bright
It turns the day from night to light.
Soon the grass will be growing
Then it will be Tyme for mowing.
And sooner Spring will be here
It's the nicest Tyme of year.
It's then the snow will turn to rain
It helps the plants to grow again.
When it's nice people will return outdoors
When they can have some fun some more.
It's baseball season and apple pie
When people and animals start to thrive.
People will swim and people will fish
At shooting stars they make a wish.
Some will go to visit with friends
On the days they hope will never end.
Some people will just enjoy the weather
When they can spend some Tyme together
Some folks will spend their Tyme with their pets
This is as good as it can get.

When the Sun Shines

Outside the sky is dim and gray
Oh, how I wish the sun would come and stay.
Outdoors the weather is nasty and cold
This drawn out weather is getting old.
I miss the green leaves, I miss the grass
I just can't wait for Winter to pass.
I look forward to spending Tyme outside
Just to work in the yard or go for a ride.
It's great to see animals out on the lawn
From late at night till it gets to be dawn.
It's great to get some warm sunshine
Just feeling the sun makes you feel so fine.
It's nice to get outside for a picnic lunch
While you have a drink and start to munch.
It's nice to get outside and fish
As you cast your line and make a wish.
When it's warm you can swim in a lake
Warm weather sure is easy to take.
It's nice to spend you day with friends
As you hope the good weather never ends.

When You're Not Here

When you're not here
And I'm alone
And I can't get
You on the phone
I start to worry
And I get frantic
Then I get scared
And I start to panic
I start to think
Something might be wrong
And then my moods
Start to rush along
Then I just need
To hear your voice
And you're not taking
My calls by choice
And that I just worried
For no reason at all
And that you'll soon
Give me a call
And let me know
That you're alright
And that you'll be
Home later tonight.

Where are you now? I wonder to myself…It's
Been so long since I heard your voice. I miss
You, I miss you so very much. It hurts to hear
You in my head. Every Tyme I think of you I
Laugh. You could make me laugh just by the
Things you use to say. We were so very close.
I wish you were here. Oh, how we'd laugh and
Have a good Tyme. I wish I could tell you just
How much I miss you. We were the very best
Of friends and as poor as church mice, but that
Never bothered us a bit. We just got by with
What we had. Remember the music? Oh, how
We Loved that music. We'd play it so loud and
So proud. We'd play it till the sun came up…
Each and every day. More than that, miss your
Carefree attitude and I miss you! I miss you
Because you were my very best friend. Nothing
Hurts more than to lose your very best friend.
But hear me out…if you are still out there…
Still…I will find you…and we will reunite and
The Pet Shop Boys will be playing so loud that
It will make your ears bleed! Just kidding…and
It will be blissful as all hell!!

Wild is the wind
On a cold Winter's day
It makes the air chilly,
But it's too cold to play.
So you stay inside
Where it is nice and warm
And too cold for Jack Frost
To do you any harm.
There are icicles everywhere you look
So stay toasty and warm with an old good book.
Stay clear from the ice
And stay clear from the snow
And try to stay comfy
Wherever you may go.
So curl up on the sofa
With your nicely warm little dog
Stay close to the fireplace
And throw on another log.
If you go outside
Take a ride on your sled
And soon you'll see your cheeks
Are rosy and also red.
You could do some ice skating
Or build a nice snow man
So just enjoy the Winter
While it's here and you still can.

My mind is like a wheel going round and around
It just speeds up and it won't slow down.
I'm so manic I feel like I'm in flight
I just can't take it, I don't feel right.
I wish I was normal just like the rest
I try to slow down my pace at best.
I want to slow down to a regular speed
To be like the rest is what I need.
I can't live right when I'm so manic
When I get like this I start to get so frantic.
I just can't stand to feel this way
I just pray that I'll be normal one day.
To help fix things I take my meds
I still feel like I wish I was dead.
Soon I'll crash and then I can sleep
Then I'll be in a depression that's deep.
I hope one day that I'll be fine
To do it I will need some help that's divine
To help me a cure I hope they'll find
But it's so hard to fix one's mind
To get help I rely on my friends
I can make do with all the Love they send.

With Just One Kiss

How I wish I was with you
I wouldn't be down and feeling so blue
You always lift my spirits high
I feel like I could touch the sky
There's so much we could do together
We wouldn't have to worry about the weather
I'll have you right by my side
And on to heaven we would ride
I would see your beautiful smile
And we could chat alone awhile
I'm so glad that you're my friend
I know we'll be together until the end
I look into your deep brown eyes
And on into heaven we would ride
I would Love to hold your hand
Holding you makes me feel so grand
Then my darling we'd make Love at last
You'd have my heartbeat beating fast
And when we're done we'd fall into bliss
It all begins with just one kiss.

You Are the Reason

You are the reason I live for, breathe for,
Try for and die for. You are the reason I'm
Alive...I live to be the reason you live for too.

You are the reason life has meaning...For
Without you the world stops spinning and
Turning.

You are the reason I get up for each day
And the reason I go to bed at night.

You are the reason I keep trying to make
A difference and keep giving of myself.

You are the reason that life makes sense,
For without you the world has no meaning.

You are the reason that I continue to try and
Not give up, even though I feel like it someTymes.

You are the reason that the world and universe
Exist...that reason is to be the center of your
Universe and revolves around you.

You in My Life

I'm so happy to have you in my life
You make every day special by just
Being you. The kind things you say
And the kind deeds that you do show
Me over and over again just how much
You care, and the Tyme we spend together
Means the world to me.

Some of the best moments we share
Are when we're just sharing a quiet
Moment together. Simple things mean
So very much. I'm so blessed to have
You in my life. I need to remember to
Tell you just how much you mean to
Me, so as not take such special Tymes
For granted.

I Love when we have a few minutes to
Share dinner or just Tyme doing some
Of the simple things during the day mean
So very much to me. It is when we are
Together that I need to be reminded to let
You know how very lucky I am to have you
As a part of my life.

SomeTymes it seems that I tell you how very
Much I Love you that it becomes trite and less
Important, but it is at these Tymes that I get to
Share my feelings that I must be reminded how
Much you do mean to me not just once in a while
But all of the Tyme we spend together...Thank
You for bringing so much joy into my life.

You Make Me Feel So Grand

You have a smile that shines so bright
You lift my soul with all your might.

You're so nice and you're so kind
Friends like you are hard to find.

You're my partner and you're my friend
You'll be with me till the end.

You're as gentle as a dove
You've helped fill my world with Love.

You're good looking, you're so fine
You're a real good friend of mine.

You lift me up when I feel blue
What a nice thing for you to do.

You make me smile when I feel sad
You calm me down when I feel mad.

You have such a wonderful smile
You always go the extra mile.

You help me when I feel morose
When I'm down you hold me close.

You have eyes as black as coal
You have such a beautiful soul.

You're so cool and you're so sweet
A Love like yours is hard to beat.

You help me if I need a hand
You always make me feel so grand.

You Make Me Smile

You make me smile
For a little while,
Thank you for being my friend.
I Love you
Yes, I Love you
I will Love you till the very end.
You'll never know dear
How much I Love you
I will Love you until the end.

You bring a smile to my face
Sadness disappears without a trace.
You always make me smile,
So now I thank you
Yes, I thank you
Thanks for making me smile for a while.
I Love you
Yes, I Love you
Thank you for making me smile for a while.

You make me smile
For a little while
So thank you for being my friend
I Love you
Oh, how I Love you
I will Love you until the end
You'll never know dear
How much I Love you,
I will Love you until the end.

You Make My Day

You make my day
In every way
Just by being you.

I just want to say
I hope you have a great day
Thank you for being you.

I can't thank you but I'll try
To help you to fly high
And enjoy you're special day.

You make my day
In every way
Just by being you.

I just want to say
I hope you have a great day
And thank you for being you.

I can't thank you but I'll try
To help you reach the sky
And make your special day.

You're the Only One

You're my world
You're my shelter from the storm
You're my friend
You're the arms that keep me warm
You're the smile
I look to save me when I'm sad
You're the only one
I turn to when I'm mad
You're the pillar
That lifts me up when I am down
You're the only one
That can turn my frown upside down
You're my strength
That makes me strong when I am weak
You're my guide
You're the one that I turn to when I'm lost and meek
You're my Love
You're the one that warms my soul
You're my direction
You're the one that helps me reach my goals.

Printed in the United States
by Baker & Taylor Publisher Services